Raintree

Threatened
Habitats

Photo Credits

• Cover: Photodisc (all) • Title page: Lonely Planet Images • Imprint page: Art Directors and Trip Photo Library, Topham Picturepoint, Bes Stock, Photodisc (left to right) • AGStockUSA: 37 (centre) • Alison Wright: 36 • ANA Press Agency: 23 • Art Directors and Trip Photo Library: 7 (bottom), 19 (centre), 21 (bottom), 24, 25 (centre), 26, 34, 35, 39 • Bes Stock: 33 • Corbis: 16, 45 • Corel: 9 (alder, groundhog, raccoon, robin, white-tailed deer, worm), 17 (bottom) • Digital Vision: 9 (mosquito) • Dr Jean-Yves Meyer/HEAR: 27 (centre) • Forest and Kim Starr/HEAR: 9 (clover) • Getty Images/HultonArchive: 11 (top), 29, 37 (top) • Great Barrier Reef Marine Park Authority: 19 (bottom) • HBL Network Photo Agency: 13 (top) • Hutchison Library: 13 (top) • • Lonely Planet Images: 5, 7 (top), 8 (top), 10, 11 (centre), 13 (centre), 14, 15 (bottom), 22, 25 (top), 27 (top), 32, 40, 41 (top), 43, 44 • North Wind Picture Archives: 31 (top) • Photobank Singapore: 15 (top), 20 • Photodisc: 4, 8 (bottom), 9 (top; all), 12, 18, 19 (top), 21 (top), 28, 31 (bottom) • R. Charles Anderson: 6 • Science Photo Library: 17 (centre), 38 • Topham Picturepoint: 17 (top), 30, 41 (bottom), 42

www.raintreepublishers.co.uk
Visit our website to find out more information about Raintree books.

To order:
☎ Phone 44 (0) 1865 888113
🖹 Send a fax to 44 (0) 1865 314091
💻 Visit the Raintree bookshop at www.raintreepublishers.co.uk
to browse our catalogue and order online.

First published in Great Britain by Raintree Publishers, Halley Court, Jordan Hill, Oxford OX2 8EJ, part of Harcourt Education Ltd. Raintree is a registered trademark of Harcourt Education Ltd.

© 2004 TIMES MEDIA PRIVATE LIMITED
Series originated and designed by
Times Media Private Limited
A member of the Times Publishing Group
1 New Industrial Road, Singapore 536196

Co-ordinating Editor   : Isabel Thomas
Writer   : Uma Sachidhanandam
Series Editor   : Katharine Brown
Project Editor   : Katharine Brown
Series Designer   : Lynn Chin Nyuk Ling
Series Picture Researchers : Susan Jane Manuel, Thomas Khoo

British Library Cataloguing in Publication Data

Threatened habitats. – (Green alert)
  1. Endangered ecosystems – Juvenile literature
  2. Endangered species – Juvenile literature
  3. Nature conservation – Juvenile literature
  333.9'516

  ISBN 1844216675
  08 07 06 05 04
  10 9 8 7 6 5 4 3 2 1

A full catalogue record for this book is available from the British Library.

Printed and bound in Malaysia

Contents

Words that appear in the glossary are printed in bold, **like this**, the first time they occur in the text.

The Earth's dry habitats

A **habitat** is the natural home of a plant or animal. Plants and animals grow in areas with suitable temperatures, moisture, soils and light. Animals live in places where they can find food easily and where competition for the same food is low. For example, giraffes and gazelles live in open woodlands. Giraffes eat twigs, fruit and leaves while grass forms the main diet of gazelles. The size of a habitat varies and can be as small as a drop of water or as large as a desert or rainforest. Larger habitats characterized by one type of vegetation are known as **biomes**.

The forest biomes

There are three main types of forest on the Earth. These are coniferous forest, deciduous forest and tropical rainforest. Coniferous forests grow mainly in North America, Europe and Asia, where winters are long and heavy snowfall can last for months. Coniferous forest trees bear cones and have needle-like leaves. Spruce, pine and fir trees are common in coniferous forests.

Deciduous forest trees include elm, oak and beech. These trees bear broad, green leaves in the spring and summer. These leaves fall off in winter. Deciduous forests are found in eastern North America, western and central Europe and north-eastern Asia.

Among the three forest types, tropical rainforests have the highest number of plant and animal species. A 0.1-square kilometre (0.038-square mile) plot of rainforest in Borneo contains over 700 species of tree. This is more than the total number of species of tree in all of North America. Rainforests thrive near the equator in South America, Africa, Asia and Australia.

In autumn, the leaves of deciduous trees turn brilliant colours of red and yellow before they fall off for winter.

Zebras grazing in the grasslands of Kenya. Zebras are members of the horse family. They live in small family groups but groups sometimes join together to form a large herd.

Grasslands

Grasslands are open, flat areas covered with grass. They extend over about a quarter of the Earth's surface and are found next to **sub-tropical** deserts or **temperate** forests on mountains. They receive 50 to 90 centimetres of rain per year. Tropical grasslands are known as savannas. Temperate grasslands include the velds of South Africa and the pampas of Argentina and Uruguay. Clover, wheat, oats and barley grow well in grasslands and provide a good source of food for animals. Some of the most common grassland animals include prairie dogs and mule deer in North America, giraffes and zebras in Africa and lions in Africa and Asia. All grasslands experience periods of **drought**.

From hot to cold

Deserts cover about one-fifth of the Earth's surface. A desert is an area that receives very little rainfall, perhaps less than 25 centimetres a year. There are four different types of desert: hot and dry, semi-arid, coastal and cold. Hot and dry deserts are the hottest, with **parched** terrain and rapid **evaporation** of water. Temperatures can reach as high as 49 °C (120 °F). Semi-arid deserts are characterized by long and dry summers, with average temperatures of 21 °C to 27 °C (70 °F to 81 °F), and little rainfall in winter. Coastal deserts are cooler because they are affected by ocean currents that lower the temperature on the land. Cold deserts are marked by big temperature differences from season to season, ranging from 38 °C (100 °F) in the summer to –12 °C (10 °F) in the winter. Polar regions are also considered to be deserts because there is no rainfall there, and any moisture in these areas is in the form of ice.

Distribution map showing the major dry biomes of the world.

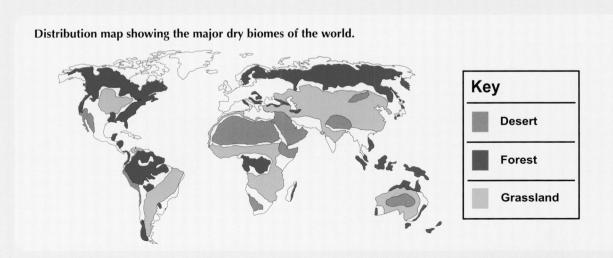

Key

Desert

Forest

Grassland

The Earth's wet habitats

More than 75 per cent of the Earth's surface is water. Ninety-seven per cent of this is salt water and the remainder is fresh water. Marine habitats are regions containing salt water, like oceans and coral reefs. Fresh water is not salty and is found in the form of ice at the north and south poles, **groundwater** and surface water in rivers, streams, lakes and ponds. Each of these wet habitats has a unique variety of animals and plants that have adapted over time to live in specific conditions. Small amounts of water are also found as water **vapour** in the atmosphere.

This triplefin is one of the most common fish found living on the coral reefs of Indonesia.

An underwater world

Oceans are enormous bodies of salt water that together cover about 360 million square kilometres (139 million square miles) of the Earth's surface. All of the world's oceans and seas form part of a continuous mass of sea water. Scientists divide this up into five oceans – the Pacific, Atlantic, Indian, Southern and Arctic – as well as many seas that are partly enclosed by land. Over 1 million species of plant and animal are known to live in the oceans and scientists estimate that a further 9 million species are yet to be discovered. Marine animals range from the huge blue whale to tiny **organisms** called plankton.

Rainforests of the ocean

Coral reefs are found in warm shallow waters in tropical areas. There are coral reefs off the coasts of Australia and Africa and around many Pacific islands. They are formed by tiny animals called coral polyps that live in **colonies**. When they die, these animals leave behind a hard, stony, branched structure made of limestone. The reefs are habitats for many organisms that rely on the corals for food and shelter. Sponges, sea slugs, oysters, clams, starfish and sea turtles make their homes in the world's coral reefs.

The Earth's surface water

All rivers and streams start on high land. The water usually comes from a spring, melting snow or **precipitation**. As the water flows downwards, it gradually joins with other small streams to form a large stream or river. This water eventually runs into the ocean or a body of water like a lake or pond. Lakes are large inland bodies of water. As the lakes are usually very deep, the Sun's rays cannot reach the bottom. Therefore, most plants in lakes are found at the edge, and these create a habitat for birds, fish and other animals. Ponds are shallow bodies of fresh water, usually not deeper than 2 metres. Because ponds are so shallow, plants may grow right across the bottom of them. These forms of surface water make up only 1 per cent of the Earth's fresh water.

Watersports like kayaking are popular on North American lakes, including Lake Union in Seattle, the USA.

Estuaries

An estuary is a coastal area where fresh water from rivers and streams mixes with salt water as it flows into the sea. Estuaries and their surrounding lands are **transitional** areas between land and sea. They are protected from the full force of ocean waves and winds by **mudflats**, sandspits and barrier islands. There are many different estuarine habitats: mangrove forests, salt and freshwater marshes, river **deltas** and wooded swamps.

Estuaries are home to a wide range of wildlife that has adapted to this type of environment. Thousands of shore and sea birds like herons and sandpipers, mammals like raccoons, skunks and opossums, fish and shellfish depend on estuarine habitats as places to live, feed and reproduce. Estuaries are also ideal places for **migratory** birds to rest on their journeys, which often take them across wide expanses of ocean.

What is an ecosystem?

An **ecosystem** is made up of a habitat, its living components (animals, plants, bacteria and fungi) and its non-living components (water, soil, air, light and heat from the Sun and **nutrients**). A healthy ecosystem is well balanced and supports many species of plant and animal.

Food chains

Food chains link together the organisms in an ecosystem. Each ecosystem is made up of many food chains. Food chains work by passing along energy from the Sun to all organisms in the chain. Plants and algae can produce their own food using the Sun's energy and are known as producers or **autotrophs**. Organisms that cannot produce their own food are known as consumers or **heterotrophs**. The consumers feed on autotrophs or other heterotrophs. There may be several consumers in the chain (known as primary, secondary and higher consumers). Decomposers such as fungi and bacteria break down dead organisms and release nutrients. With the help of decomposers, energy and nutrients are continually recycled through the ecosystem.

*Fungi growing on the trunk of a tree. Fungi do not have **chlorophyll** so they cannot make their own food. Instead they feed off other organisms.*

Parts of a food chain

Here is an example of a simple food chain.

Grass   Rabbit   Fox

The Sun's light energy is used by grass to power the process of **photosynthesis**. This allows the grass to store the Sun's energy as chemical energy. This chemical energy is passed on to the rabbits when they eat the grass and then to foxes when they eat the rabbits. Nutrients are finally returned to the soil when a rabbit or fox dies and its carcass is decomposed by bacteria.

Tipping the scales

If one part of an ecosystem becomes unbalanced, the entire habitat is threatened. If there is insufficient sunlight, water or nutrients in the soil, the plants in an ecosystem will not grow. If the plants die, the animals that depend on them for food will die. Secondary consumers that rely on those animals for food will also die. As a result, the food chain becomes more and more unbalanced and the ecosystem is likely to collapse.

The ecosystem of Lake Pontchartrain in the USA is under threat. Fertilizers spread on nearby cropland have been washed into the lake in rain water and have led to an increase in the growth of algae. The spread of algae stops sunlight from reaching the aquatic plants and reduces the lake's oxygen supply. As the plants die, small fish that depend on these plants also begin to die. In turn, larger fish that feed off the smaller fish, and which also need oxygen in the water, either die or are forced to leave to find new food supplies.

Mapping a food web

The way that plants and animals in an ecosystem are connected through food chains is called a food web. A food web shows how plants and animals depend on each other for survival. If one plant or animal dies, the entire food web is affected. Many food chains may make up a food web. This is a simple example. Each colour shows a single food chain.

Raccoon   Robin   Groundhog   Mosquito

Worm   Clover   Alder   White-tailed Deer

Measuring a threatened habitat

Before researchers can decide if a habitat is threatened, they must conduct a survey of the area. First, they collect information and use this to estimate the **biodiversity** in an area. They then compare their findings with similar habitats. Measurements of the number and distribution of species help scientists to decide which habitats are most threatened. Several different survey methods are used by researchers to look at different habitats.

Surveying habitats

A line transect involves counting all of the species living along a measured straight line. This is usually measured in units of 10 metres. Markings are made at every metre. The species are identified and counted along that metre and then recorded. Line transects can be carried out on the land and in fresh or sea water.

Scientists also use quadrats to measure the biodiversity in **terrestrial** habitats like mudflats and grasslands. Quadrats are square wooden frames measuring 1 metre by 1 metre. They are randomly placed on the ground and all species found within the quadrat are recorded on survey sheets.

Sometimes researchers simply look out for and write down the animals and plants that they can see in a habitat. This is often done for mammals and birds. Birds can also be detected by listening out for their calls. Animals such as small mammals and reptiles can be caught and identified using traps and nets are used to catch fish in streams and lakes. The animals and fish are not harmed and are released after they have been identified and counted.

Bird watching is one way of counting how many bird species live in a particular habitat like Everglades National Park in Florida.

Mapping habitats

Researchers use a variety of techniques to help them study habitats. These include satellite images and aerial photographs. Geographic Information Systems (GIS) technology helps scientists to locate these images accurately. Images from different dates can be compared to show changes in the location, size and state of a habitat. Endangered habitats that need protection can then be identified. Scientists can also use these techniques to detect threats to habitats, such as forest fires, and human activities like building, mining and clearing the land for agriculture.

A satellite image showing an overview of a forest fire in the Pike National Forest, south of Denver, Colorado, in 2000. The fire spread over 348 square kilometres (135 square miles) of forested land.

Colourful butterfly fish in the coral reefs of the Red Sea.

Indicator species

Scientists use certain animal and plant species like lichens, insect larvae, clams and fish to investigate the health of the environment. Such species are very sensitive to any changes in their habitat and often leave clues about the state of the area they live in. They are therefore known as indicator species. The butterfly fish is an indicator species that is used to monitor the state of coral reefs. Butterfly fish feed directly on the live tissue of corals and are very sensitive to changing conditions in the reefs. If the corals are unhealthy because of pollution in the water, the fish will swim to more healthy areas of the reef and feed on the corals there. Therefore, a decline in butterfly fish populations gives scientists an early indication of the condition of the reef.

The Earth's 'hotspots'

Biologists at Conservation International, an international organization that is concerned for the Earth's habitats, have identified 25 of the world's most biologically rich areas. These special areas, called 'hotspots', cover just 1.4 per cent of the Earth's surface but are home to more than 60 per cent of all known species. They include Madagascar and the Atlantic Forest in South America. These are all extremely endangered places. It is estimated that many of these hotspots have lost about 90 per cent of their vegetation and a very large proportion of the species that once lived there since people began to settle in these areas.

Human activity and degrading habitats

Human activity is the major cause of habitat destruction. Urbanization, logging, grazing, mining and leisure activities place a tremendous amount of stress on surrounding habitats. These daily activities can degrade, or reduce the richness of, the Earth's precious habitats and eventually destroy them.

Farmers in Indonesia clear land for agricultural use by burning trees and grasses.

Clearing habitats

People clear land to grow crops, raise animals for food and build homes or industries that make the products we need. In Australia, more than 6000 square kilometres (2316 square miles) of bushland are cleared every year for cattle grazing or for urban development. This land clearing kills more than 2 million mammals, 9 million birds and 100 million reptiles each year. As a result, many animal species in Australia are in decline and one in five bird species is at risk of **extinction**.

Coastal habitats like salt marshes and mangroves are often cleared to build tourist resorts and ponds to breed fish. In the USA, over 50 per cent of the wetlands that were there 200 years ago have been drained or filled in so the land could be converted for people to live on.

Losing habitats

The greatest destruction of habitats has occurred in the past 150 years. During this time, the world population has increased from around 1 billion in 1850 to almost 6.4 billion in 2004. As populations grow, so does the need for land. These ever-increasing demands mean that natural resources are used up and eventually destroyed. In 49 out of 61 countries in Africa and Asia, over 50 per cent of the **native** habitat has been lost. On island countries where land space is very limited and where there are many people, much of the original habitat has disappeared.

Right: Reclaimed land in Singapore. The island's land area grew by 42 square kilometres (16 square miles) between 1992 and 2002. In land reclamation, coral reefs and seagrass beds are sometimes covered with sand to reclaim the area from the sea.

Left: Portuguese fishermen pulling in their huge nets. Since the 1990s, their annual fish catch has slowly declined due mainly to reduced fish populations.

Driven to extinction

The dodo bird of Mauritius, an island in the Indian Ocean, was hunted to extinction by humans by 1681. Over 300 years later, botanists wondered why there were no young *Calvaria* trees growing on the island. All the island's *Calvaria* trees were estimated to be at least 300 years old and by the 1970s only thirteen were left. Scientists discovered that *Calvaria* seeds need to pass through the dodo's digestive system before new seedlings can sprout. Today, scientists are hoping that turkeys may be able to replace the role of the dodo in this process.

Overexploiting habitats

Farming and hunting lead to habitat degradation and loss. Today, we are removing more animals and plants than ever before. Marine habitats have been particularly devastated by overfishing. Trawling is a method that uses huge nets to catch fish. This has severely reduced fish populations in many of the world's seas. In the Black Sea in Central Asia, fishing began on a large scale in the 1970s. Since then, fish like tuna, mackerel and bluefish have been much reduced in number and the monk seal has become extinct.

Human activity and fragmentation

The break-up, or fragmentation, of habitats occurs when large continuous **tracts** of land are split up into separate smaller parts. These parts can no longer support a full range of species and become isolated from others of their own kind. Fragmentation usually happens when people construct roads, build houses or clear small pockets of land for agriculture.

Transport

The construction of transport **infrastructure** cuts up large areas of land into smaller patches. Since the beginning of the 20th century, habitats across the world have become increasingly fragmented as bigger transport systems are built. The construction of the Trans-Canada Highway in the 1960s fragmented vast expanses of land, including the Bow River Valley in south-central Canada. This has since had a devastating impact on the wildlife living in the valley. It has led to an increase in the death of animals, like elk, deer and wolves, through collisions with motor vehicles. It has also restricted the natural movements of wildlife in the valley.

A bull bison risks being run down as it crosses a busy road in Yellowstone National Park in the USA.

Urbanization

Over the centuries, urbanization has destroyed various habitats to build towns and cities for people to live in. Today, as the demand for living space continues to increase, more and more open land is being used to build houses, shopping centres, office complexes and industrial parks. Such construction isolates and fragments any remaining parts of the original habitat. By the early 1990s, urban sprawl in California had destroyed 90 per cent of the original coastal ecosystem, leaving the remaining 10 per cent severely fragmented.

Dirt roads leading to an open-cut iron ore mine have fragmented large areas of land in Western Australia. The development of such roads can increase the value of the land and attract development for recreation and industry. This leads to more fragmentation.

Hardened lava covers part of a coastal road on the island of Hawaii, also known as Big Island.

Natural fragmentation

Not all habitat fragmentation is caused by human actions. Hurricanes and tornadoes can damage areas of vegetation and cause land disturbance. Earthquake activity can break land apart at fault lines and isolate habitats. **Lava** from volcanic eruptions can cover parts of the landscape and break up habitats into smaller segments. Floods and drought can also isolate patches of land, fragmenting it temporarily or permanently.

Vanishing forests

The forested areas in the county of Warwickshire in the UK have been fragmented and reduced in area by the building of roads, agricultural areas, houses and paths since AD 400. By 1960, only tiny patches of fragmented forest remained so many species could no longer survive. There was not enough food in these small isolated areas to support them and now these habitats are under serious threat of vanishing altogether.

Alien invasions

Humans are the most mobile species on the Earth. When they travel from place to place, they often transport other species with them, bringing in **alien species**. While the most drastic devastation occurs on small islands, alien introductions into large land masses have also had a huge impact.

Trees in southern USA are covered completely by the kudzu vine. A number of non-native ornamental plants including the kudzu vine have spread into natural landscapes.

The newcomers

Some species have invaded new habitats on their own, for example when stopping off on a migration route. Others, such as rats, have been transported by people to habitats around the world unintentionally, as unwanted passengers on cargo ships.

Most alien species, however, have been intentionally introduced into new habitats by settlers and colonizers. These people brought along animals and even plants to remind them of their former homes or to provide them with a good source of familiar food. The kudzu vine from Japan was introduced to the USA in 1876 as an ornamental plant and was widely planted in the 1940s to stop soil erosion. It grows very quickly and can kill entire forests by smothering trees and shrubs. Today, it covers thousands of square kilometres in the southern USA.

A new species on the block

When an alien species appears in a new habitat, the native species there often cannot respond quickly to the new threat. This is because their defence mechanisms have developed over time to protect them from very specific organisms. But the alien species may not encounter any natural enemies in its new habitat as it has left behind the **predators**, diseases and environmental changes that kept its population under control. In this new environment, the alien species is free to grow and spread at an alarming rate. When this happens, the alien species becomes an **invasive species**.

Zebra mussels were introduced to the Great Lakes region in the USA in the 1980s. They are now threatening the survival of many native species, including freshwater clams. Hundreds of zebra mussels can grow on one freshwater clam, making it difficult for the clam to move around and survive.

Survival of the fittest

An invasive species can adapt almost immediately to a new environment and quickly start to compete for food and space. If a native species is not strong enough to resist, the alien species spreads quickly and displaces the native species or even pushes it to extinction. Today, approximately 18 per cent of endangered mammals in Australia and the Americas and 20 per cent of the world's birds are threatened by alien species.

The eggs of a female cane toad. The female cane toad was introduced to Australia in 1935. It can lay up to 30,000 eggs per year compared with the 1000 laid by native Australian frogs.

Monocultures

Alien plants often create a landscape in which one species completely, or almost completely, predominates. Such a landscape is known as a **monoculture**. A good example is purple loosestrife (*right*), a plant from Europe that now blankets about 1600 square kilometres (600 square miles) of North America. Such monocultures have little ecological value and greatly reduce the natural biodiversity of an area.

Natural environmental changes

Throughout history, the Earth's climate has varied between periods of warmth and cold. Through natural climate change, different habitats have come and gone. As recently as 14,000 years ago, much of northern America and northern Europe lay under ice sheets. Today, most ice is found only near the north and south poles. Habitats never stay the same; they are constantly changing and **evolving** with the climate. Over a period of years, open water areas can change to woodlands while seabeds turn into deserts as water levels drop. In Wadi Zeuglodon in the Egyptian Sahara Desert, fossilized bodies of prehistoric whales can be found littering the desert floor. Forty million years ago, this desert was the Tethys Sea.

Surviving the weather

Storms and hurricanes destroy patches of forest, mangrove and even coral reef every year. Continuous drought can change grasslands into dust bowls, where few plants or animals can survive. Floods caused by rains can destroy river, stream and pond habitats by causing overflow and waterlogging and extreme flooding can alter habitats by erosion. Wildfires caused by lightning destroy huge areas of grassland and forest each year.

Hurricanes sweeping the Caribbean can have devastating effects on surrounding habitats.

Animal behaviour

Animals can change their own environments by their natural behaviour. Elephants in Africa and Asia eat all of the leaves from trees and bushes and pull up trees from the ground. Natural fires may then prevent the trees from growing back. This has created grasslands where there was once wooded forest. In the UK, large sheep populations overgraze the vegetation on hillsides. When grass is overgrazed, its roots are then too short to trap and absorb rain water. The excess water drains off the hills too quickly and topsoil is washed into rivers and reservoirs, killing wildlife.

An elephant in northern Kenya looks for food.

Geological factors

Volcanic eruptions can radically change landscapes by covering land with molten lava. Large eruptions also send up clouds of smoke and dust into the atmosphere and block out sunlight which is needed by plants to make food by photosynthesis. On 18 May 1980, Mount St Helens in the USA erupted, killing an estimated 24,000 wild animals and destroying 240 square kilometres (93 square miles) of forest as well as a large lake.

Today, the habitat around Mount St Helens is still struggling to recover from the volcanic eruption that happened in 1980.

Coral bleaching

In 2002, three-fifths of the Great Barrier Reef in Australia were affected by coral **bleaching**. Scientists blamed it on a rise in water temperatures resulting from the natural warm water phenomenon known as *El Niño* that occurs once every three to five years. Higher water temperatures put the coral under stress. As a result, the zooxanthellae, or algae, in the coral's tissue is released, bleaching the coral white. If the bleaching continues for a long time, the coral reef eventually dies.

Threatened habitats and ecosystems

When an ecosystem is healthy, there is a balance between the wildlife and the resources available. When one part of a balanced ecosystem is destroyed or removed, it affects the other parts, causing the ecosystem to decline eventually. Ecosystems do not exist in isolation. Chemical and physical interactions take place between neighbouring ecosystems, such as between mountain forests and wetlands and between coral reefs, mangroves and seagrass beds. So destroying one part of an ecosystem can also have negative effects on surrounding habitats.

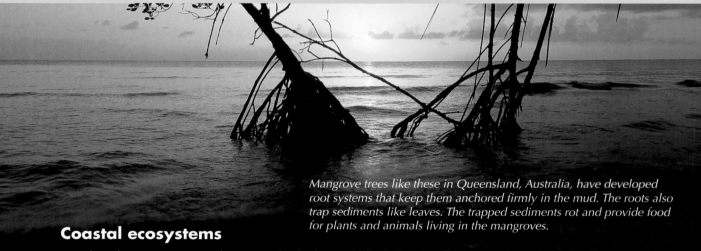

Mangrove trees like these in Queensland, Australia, have developed root systems that keep them anchored firmly in the mud. The roots also trap sediments like leaves. The trapped sediments rot and provide food for plants and animals living in the mangroves.

Coastal ecosystems

Coral reefs, mangroves and seagrass beds depend on each other for survival. When one of these coastal ecosystems is threatened, the others are, too. Seagrass beds and mangroves depend on the sheltering effects of coral reefs to grow. When coral reefs are destroyed, there is nothing to prevent huge waves from crashing on to the shore and damaging the coastal plants. Mangroves and seagrasses also rely on calcium from coral reefs. When the calcium is broken down, the **sediments** build up and create the right environment for the mangroves and seagrasses.

Likewise, the removal of mangrove forests directly affects coral reef ecosystems. The roots and trees of mangroves protect coral reefs by stopping sediment from rivers and streams from moving out into the sea. This is important as coral reefs can only develop in clear, warm waters; any sediment would cloud the water, settle on the corals and smother them. Mangrove forests also create nutrient-rich waters that act as nurseries for young fish and other marine organisms that eventually make their home in the coral reefs. The coral reef at Tamandare in Brazil is dying because the mangrove forest there has been destroyed

Water gushing down a river floods the surrounding land.

Forests and wetlands

Forests collect and hold rain water. The rain water then flows downstream at a gentle rate to reach rivers, streams and wetlands. Tree roots bind soil together, but when a forest is removed, water flows off the bare land very rapidly. There is also an increase in the amount of sediment and nutrients washed downstream. This can lead to increased algae growth in downstream habitats. The greater sediment load in the water can also threaten low-lying wetland habitats by contaminating water supplies.

A chain of wetlands

During the harsh winter months in the northern hemisphere, about 55 species of wading bird fly to warmer climates in the southern hemisphere along the East Asian-Australasian Flyway. This flyway stretches across twenty countries and covers thousands of wetlands. The birds stop at the wetlands to feed and rest during their journey. This flyway is considered the most threatened in the world because many countries along it have lost or are losing their wetland habitats to development. Japan has lost nearly 40 per cent of its wetlands since the 1950s while Australia has lost about half of its wetlands in the last 200 years. Scientists fear that the loss of even one of the flyway wetlands could have a disastrous effect on the migration patterns of the birds.

Depleted coral reefs in the Philippines

The Philippines is a group of 7100 islands in Southeast Asia. It is bordered by the Philippine Sea to the east, the Celebes Sea to the south and the South China Sea to the west and north. The total area of the Philippines is 300,000 square kilometres (115,830 square miles). The country has more than a quarter of the region's coral reefs, second only to Indonesia.

A small boat takes divers into the clear, blue waters off the eastern coast of Mindoro Island. Today, less than 4 per cent, or 1080 square kilometres (420 square miles), of the coral reefs in the Philippines are in a good condition.

The heart of the coral triangle

The Philippines has about 27,000 square kilometres (10,500 square miles) of coral reefs. These reefs are located at the centre of the coral triangle, the most diverse marine habitat on the Earth. The reefs contain an estimated 400 species of coral, 971 species of algae and over 2000 species of fish. The plants and animals harvested from these reefs are thought to provide 50 per cent of the **protein** eaten by the Filipino population.

Fish caught in the reefs of the Philippines is a key food source for the country's population.

Under attack

Today, the coral reefs of the Philippines are among the most threatened in Southeast Asia. Over 80 per cent of the reefs are threatened by overfishing. Large coastal communities and rapid population growth mean that there is more fishing in order to feed these communities.

Destructive fishing methods have damaged many of the reefs. Commercial fishers use poisons like cyanide to stun and capture reef fish. This harms not only the fish but also the corals and other creatures in the water. Fishers also use dynamite to kill fish in an area. This reduces nearby coral to rubble.

Overfishing is not the only cause. Extensive coastal development, agriculture and the clearing of forests have also created areas of bare soil. This is washed downstream into the ocean and on to the coral reefs. The dirt, silt and sand turn the water cloudy and smother the coral.

What is happening?

Coral reefs are important to the marine ecosystem because they produce oxygen. As the Philippine reefs are damaged or destroyed, the amount of oxygen available to other sea creatures declines. Fish populations in the area have also fallen as they move to find food elsewhere. Animals like cuttlefish that **spawn** on the reefs lose places where they can breed and lay eggs safely. Other animals, such as sea urchins and clams, cannot move away and die on the reef. Any remaining mangrove habitats are also affected because the healthy coral reefs that protect them from the sea have been destroyed.

Under threat

The coral reefs of Southeast Asia cover nearly 100,000 square kilometres (38,610 square miles) and make up almost 34 per cent of the world total. They have the highest levels of marine biodiversity on the Earth and contain the greatest number of coral reef fish, **molluscs** and **crustaceans** of all reefs worldwide. The Southeast Asian coral reefs are also the world's most threatened reefs, with more than 80 per cent of them at risk.

Threatened habitats and plants

Habitat destruction can affect plants in a number of ways. Plant populations respond to threats by either thriving, adapting or diminishing. Plants play an important role in ecosystems as primary producers and they are at the start of every food chain. If plants are removed or cannot adapt to change, food chains collapse and habitats become endangered.

Regeneration

Many plants regenerate after a wildfire has damaged their habitat. The destruction of a natural habitat is an important part of the life cycle of some plants, especially in grassland and forest ecosystems.

In grasslands, fire removes the dead stems and leaves of plants above the ground, without killing the roots below. These plants can grow again from either their roots or their seeds. This cycle of burning and regrowth helps stop the grassland ecosystem from changing into a forest habitat because the regular fires prevent the growth of shrubs and trees.

In temperate forests such as those in Europe, wildfires enhance the nutrient levels of the soil. The ash that is left behind forms a natural fertilizer and helps the flowering and fruiting of new plants. The intense heat also causes pine cones to open and drop their seeds into the nutrient-enriched soil.

Natural tree-fall in a forest, caused by storms or lightning, allows more light and rainfall on to the forest floor and stimulates the growth of many herbs and woody plants. Young trees also take the opportunity to shoot up into the gap and begin to grow rapidly.

Forest fires like this one in Dartmoor, the UK, can help forest ecosystems to remain healthy. Many plant species depend on occasional fires so that their flowers or seeds can grow.

Many tree species are able to adapt to changes in the surrounding environment as long as these changes are gradual.

The devastating results of a forest fire that swept across north-east Spain. Not all plant and tree species are able to survive forest fires.

Adaptation

Other plants cope with environmental changes and stress by adapting. Research has shown that plants accumulate proline, an **amino acid**, during times of drought. Proline protects the plant cells and proteins against the effects of high temperatures and lack of water in a dry, hot climate. Plants and trees can also extend or reduce their range of growth on mountains and at higher altitudes according to temperature changes. With the current rise in the Earth's temperatures, scientists believe the natural growth range of trees such as the Douglas fir, western hemlock, Ponderosa pine and Engelmann spruce in the USA will probably shift northwards and up-slope to higher altitudes.

Reduction

However, many plant species cannot adapt successfully to habitat change. Currently, at least one in eight plants worldwide is threatened with extinction due to competition from the introduction of alien species and loss of habitat. The *Moringa hildebrandtii* of Madagascar is now extinct in the wild because its natural habitat has been destroyed. It survives today only as a decorative garden plant and on farms where it is **cultivated** as a source of nutritional supplements.

The end of the line

Many plants around the world stand as lone survivors because they no longer reproduce. At San Francisco's Golden Gate National Recreation Area, the *Presidio manzanita* species exists as a single remaining plant. Cuttings have been taken from the shrub to make new plants, but this is not a natural form of reproduction and the new plants cannot reproduce themselves. So when the parent plant dies, the species will be considered extinct.

Hawaii's invasive species

The Hawaiian chain of islands covers a total area of 16,760 square kilometres (6470 square miles) in the Central Pacific Ocean. The islands have existed for about 70 million years. Because Hawaii is situated in the middle of the ocean, it developed a rich and varied wildlife that cannot be found anywhere else on the Earth. In the last few centuries, other plants and mammals have been introduced to Hawaii's eight islands. Today, the biggest environmental threat to Hawaiian habitats is the introduction of alien species.

Natural wildlife

Hawaii is famous for its rich plant life, of which many are native to the chain of islands. Biologists believe that Hawaii's natural vegetation evolved from a small number of plants. Today, the islands have over 1140 different plant species. About 90 per cent of these grow nowhere else in the world. Forests and woodlands cover 43 per cent of Hawaii. Common native trees that can be found all over the islands include the *ohia*, *hala* and *koa*. Grasslands and pasture make up 25 per cent of the land.

Native animals to Hawaii are limited to insects, land snails, bats and birds. The islands are home to over 5000 native species of insect and land snail. Native Hawaiian birds include the honeycreeper and the nene, the state bird of Hawaii.

Kauai Island is the oldest of Hawaii's main islands. As the island has a lot of green vegetation, it is also known as the Garden Isle.

The arrival of people

The islands of Hawaii were geographically isolated until Polynesian people from other Pacific islands arrived in AD 400. As they settled in Hawaii, they brought plants and animals with them. These included sweet potatoes, sugar cane, dogs and pigs. When Europeans and Americans arrived on the islands in the 1700s and 1800s, they introduced more animal and plant species. Many of these settlers cleared and burned much of the vegetation. This destruction made it easier for the introduced plants to grow. Today, about 20 to 50 new non-native species are introduced to Hawaii by people each year.

Left: The strawberry guava (Psidium cattleianum) was introduced into Hawaii as a fruit crop in the early 1800s. It has crowded out a local endangered species, Cyanea superba, by forming dense undergrowth. As a result, Cyanea superba is now limited to two areas of less than 1000 square metres each on Oahu Island.

Alien domination and death of the natives

More than 4500 alien plant species have been brought to Hawaii. These invasive species grow easily and reproduce quickly in their new environment, often taking the place of less aggressive native plants as they compete for sunlight and space. Some invasive species grow so large they do not allow other plants to grow. The velvet tree, *Miconia calvescens*, is one of the most threatening invasive plant species in Hawaii. Many of these new plants are specially grown for sale to tourists and locals who buy them to decorate their homes and workplaces. As a result, about 9 per cent of Hawaii's native plants have already become extinct and 40 per cent more are under threat.

Velvet trees crowd out native Hawaiian plants. The velvet tree grows 4 to 15 metres tall and produces a purple fruit that contains many seeds.

Stopping the threat

The people of Hawaii have come together to form the Hawaii State Island Invasive Species Committee. The society consists of private and governmental organizations as well as concerned citizens. The society aims to control the spread of invasive plants through measures such as replanting native trees and laws to prevent the import of new invasive species.

Threatened habitats and animals

An animal depends on its habitat for food, water, shelter and to reproduce. When a habitat is destroyed or damaged, some animals such as birds and large mammals are able to move to another habitat but many cannot. If a habitat is destroyed, entire populations of animals can become locally extinct.

Genetic inbreeding

The fragmentation, or break-up, of habitats into smaller pieces isolates animals in small islands and they lose contact with other members of their species. Smaller animal populations are more likely to suffer from **inbreeding**. As there are fewer choices of mate, animals are forced to breed with genetically similar relatives. This inbreeding reduces **genetic diversity** and the population becomes less adaptable to changes in the environment. The animals are also more vulnerable to disease and may have problems reproducing.

Cheetah populations in Kenya have suffered greatly from fragmentation. The remaining isolated populations have inbred and they are now more likely to catch diseases and have smaller litters.

Animal migration

When faced with loss of habitat, many animals try to find another suitable habitat. As they migrate or move between habitats, they may be attacked by predators or suffer harsh environmental conditions and even starvation. Once they reach a suitable habitat, they must compete with the animals already living there. While some animals will tolerate new arrivals, others will fight to defend their territory.

Reduced home ranges

Most animals live in a limited area known as their **home range**. This is where they find their food and spend most of their time. When a habitat is destroyed or reduced, many animals are left without a suitable home range or one that is large enough. A smaller habitat may not be able to support all of the original animal species, especially large ones that need a lot of space. This reduction in habitat increases competition for the remaining natural resources and has disastrous effects on some animals. Black bears in North America are often forced to leave their reduced home range in forest and woodland habitats to search for food. Increasingly, they travel into nearby towns to scavenge for food or attack livestock. This has put them into conflict with people, who fear the bears may attack them or their children.

A male antelope defends its territory from another male that is either trying to get its own territorial land or expand the size of the territory that it already has.

Edge effects

As habitats are fragmented into smaller patches, a larger part of each patch will be next to a different type of habitat. Land that is in the middle of a forest is very different from the land at its edge. The 'edge effect', where habitats meet, can be extremely harmful to animals. If an animal roams too close to the edge of its protective habitat, it can be quickly caught by predators from the neighbouring habitat. Some animal species that thrive within their own habitat cannot compete with species that invade the edge of the habitat. Other animals are better adapted to living across the boundary of two different ecosystems.

Fragmentation of Illinois' prairies

Illinois is located in north-central USA. It is bordered by the Mississippi River in the west and Lake Michigan in the north-east. Illinois is largely an area of flat or gently rolling plains covered by wildflowers and tall prairie grasses such as big bluestem. It is nicknamed the Prairie State.

Settling on the land

Early European settlers first arrived in the area in the late 1600s. They found that the prairie soil there was extremely fertile and immediately began to convert the prairies into agricultural land. Since their arrival, much of the state's prairie land has been cleared to grow crops like corn and soya beans and to raise livestock like pigs. Land has also been cleared to make way for residential and commercial development. Prairies once covered approximately 90,000 square kilometres (35,000 square miles) of central and northern Illinois. Today, less than 9.3 square kilometres (3.6 square miles) of high-quality prairie remains. Most of this land is fragmented.

*Much of Illinois' prairies has been converted into agricultural land. This storage facility can hold up to 1.7 million **bushels** of corn.*

Disappearance of prairie animals

The conversion and fragmentation of the prairies have been so extensive that many prairie animals have been forced to move to new habitats or have reduced in number. The bison has disappeared from the Illinois landscape. Bison are grazers that feed on tall grasses. They live in large herds that need huge areas of open grassland or they will exhaust the supply of plants that they eat. As settlers changed the prairies into farmland and built towns and roads, the home range of the bison was reduced until the animals could no longer survive. By the 1820s, these large animals had disappeared from the prairies. Since the settlement of Illinois began, eighteen prairie species, including the bison, have become extinct and now 127 more species are threatened or endangered.

Many bison were killed for food and for their hides by early European settlers.

Prairie chickens and shrinking genes

The prairie chicken population in Illinois fell from 25,000 in 1933 to less than 50 by 1993. Fragmentation of their habitat has reduced the area in which they can find food and has caused the isolation of small groups of prairie chickens. This means these different groups have not been able to meet and breed with each other. This reduces their genetic diversity, leading to a decline in their ability to resist disease, a shorter life span and fewer eggs being laid. In 1998, researchers calculated that the genetic diversity of present-day prairie chickens was 30 per cent lower than that of their ancestors. The successful hatching of eggs also fell, from more than 90 per cent in the 1960s to 74 per cent by the 1990s.

Prairie pollinators

Insects like the monarch butterfly (*right*) and honeybees are important to prairie ecosystems because they are responsible for the **pollination** of many prairie plants. These pollinators have been seriously affected by the conversion and fragmentation of the prairies as they rely on an undisturbed habitat to find food and shelter.

   As the prairies have become more and more fragmented, the small islands where native plants grow are sometimes too far away from one another for the pollinators to reach them. This leads to the death of the pollinators. It also means that pollen is not always spread from one plant to another so plants cannot reproduce. The conversion of the land has led many wildflowers, such as asters and milkweed, to die out. This results in further starvation of the pollinators.

Threatened habitats and people

Even in prehistoric times, people killed animals for food and cut down trees for fuel and to cook. As there were so few people living throughout the world at that time, their activities had little impact on the surrounding habitats. Most of the human destruction of habitats and ecosystems has taken place in the last 150 years, during which time the human population has grown from 1 billion to over 6 billion. It is estimated that the number of people living on the Earth will reach 9 billion by 2050. As we use more and more **fossil fuels**, minerals, metals and food, we place increasing stress on the world's habitats and resources. Loss of habitats and biodiversity will, in turn, threaten our food, water and energy and our lifestyles.

Lost ways of life

Many **indigenous** peoples, such as those living in South America's Amazon rainforest, exist only on the resources found in their local habitat. When these resources are destroyed, the indigenous people lose their homes and their sources of food. They are often forced to move to other areas for shelter and food, which can lead to further destruction of the surrounding ecosystem. It also means the loss of a way of life and of the very special skills and knowledge that these people have.

A Hmong woman selling herbal medicines. Many of these medicines come from the rainforests of Laos in Indochina.

Falling fish supplies

Most of the food taken directly from the wild is from aquatic sources like oceans, rivers and lakes. We harvest 91 million tons of fish and shellfish per year from marine sources and 17 million tons from fresh water sources. Fish account for roughly one-fifth of all animal protein in the human diet and around 1 billion people rely on fish as their main source of protein. The over-exploitation of fishing resources by commercial fisheries is leading to the decline of many fish species. In North America alone, 82 species are at some risk of extinction. The total worldwide supply of fish began to decline in the mid-1990s. If this decline continues, humans will be deprived of an essential source of protein. People living in coastal communities who work in the fishing industry or related businesses will also lose their livelihood.

Fishermen catching tuna in the Pacific Ocean.

Losing more than just plants

Plants provide oxygen for people and animals to breathe and they are an important source of food. They also provide us with most of our medicines. Over 7000 different types of medicine contain ingredients made from plants. These ingredients include aspirin from the willow family. Fewer than 1 per cent of the world's plant species have been studied to find out if they can be used as medicine. We are in danger of losing important medicines before they have even been discovered because many plants and their habitats are being destroyed.

Saving ecosystems to save money

In 2002, scientists estimated that destroying habitats costs the world about US$250 billion each year in cash terms. This is because natural ecosystems provide ready-made protection from storms and floods, regulate the climate, keep water resources clean and allow **sustainable** harvesting of plants and animals. The scientists based their findings on the conversion of freshwater marshes in Canada into agricultural land. They calculated that the area would be worth about 60 per cent more if the wetlands had been left as they were and used only for recreation.

The shrinking Aral Sea

The Aral Sea lies in south-west Kazakhstan and northern Uzbekistan in Central Asia. It is a saltwater lake. Water from the Amu Darya and Syr' Darya rivers flows into the Aral Sea but there are no rivers or streams flowing out of it. For centuries, the lake has provided water for the people living in the surrounding areas and for agriculture.

Growing cotton

In the early 1960s, there was rapid development of cotton farming in the plains of Uzbekistan and Kazakhstan. Water was taken from the two rivers to **irrigate** the cotton crops. As cotton became an important export, more and more land around the Aral Sea was used to grow the crop. By the 1980s, about 120 cubic kilometres (29 cubic miles) of water was being taken from the rivers each year. About 90 per cent of this water was used for agriculture. As a result, the amount of water that reached the Aral Sea dropped drastically and many parts of the lake dried up.

Women picking cotton in northern Uzbekistan. Although the water levels of the Aral Sea have decreased greatly, farmers continue to take water from the lake to use on their crops.

This abandoned boat was once docked in a port along the Aral Sea. Towns that were once ports along the Aral Sea are now many kilometres away from the lake's waters. In some places, shorelines have backed up by up to 120 kilometres (75 miles).

A ruined economy

As the Aral Sea shrank, its water became saltier because there was less fresh water to dilute the salt in the lake. Today, the level of salt in the lake is the same as that of the open ocean. As the **salinity** of the water increased, most of the fish and invertebrate species living in the lake died out. Annual fish catches have fallen from 48,000 tonnes a year to zero. Commercial fisheries that once lined the lake have shut down and people have had to find other jobs or move away. Many of the Aral Sea's surrounding habitats have also disappeared, including the fragile tugai forests that local people relied upon for firewood.

Health problems

The people living in the area suffer from serious health problems like cancer, tuberculosis and kidney and liver disease. These problems are the result of pesticides and fertilizers that farmers sprayed on the cotton fields. The chemicals in them have drained underground and seeped back into the river system, polluting the water in the lake with high contents of metals like zinc and manganese. Not only is the water too salty to drink, it is contaminated with these metals. In Karakalpakstan, Uzbekistan, there has been a 3000 per cent increase in **chronic** bronchitis since the early 1980s. The death rate for infants and children here is one of the highest in the world.

The dried-up lake bed is lined with layers of salt and agricultural chemicals. Strong winds carry an estimated annual total of 15 to 75 million tonnes of dust, salt and chemicals and deposit them up to 250 kilometres (155 miles) away. Traces of Aral salt have been found in the fertile Fergana Valley in Georgia on the Black Sea coast. These dust clouds trigger asthma attacks, breathing difficulties and eye and skin irritations. They also contaminate fresh water sources.

Split in two

The Aral Sea once covered an area of about 68,000 square kilometres (26,255 square miles). It was the fourth largest inland body of water in the world. Since the 1960s, its area has shrunk by more than half. Today, the Aral Sea is split into two bodies of water – the northern Small Aral and the southern Large Aral. Some scientists believe that the Aral Sea could disappear completely by 2015.

Saving the Earth's biodiversity

In 1992, world leaders met in Rio de Janeiro, Brazil. This meeting became known as the Earth Summit. During the conference, over 150 governments signed the **Convention** on Biological Diversity. This Convention was the first global agreement on the conservation and sustainable use of the Earth's biodiversity. Today, a total of 187 countries have signed up to the agreement.

The goals of the Convention

At the conference, the world leaders agreed upon the three main goals of the Convention. These goals are the conservation of biological diversity, the sustainable use of the Earth's resources and the fair sharing of benefits brought about by the use of these resources. The world leaders also acknowledged that the Convention would only be successful if all three goals were met.

Women working in the rice fields of northern Vietnam. By attending weekly 'farmer field schools', rice farmers in Asian countries like Vietnam and Cambodia have learned how the rice ecosystem works. As a result, they have been able to increase the amount of rice grown while reducing the use of insecticides that harm the ecosystem. To date, about 2 million farmers have benefited from this approach.

2010 – The Global Diversity Challenge

Since 1992, the Global Environment Facility (GEF), the financial body of the Convention, has contributed more than US$1 billion for biodiversity projects throughout the world. Despite these efforts, the threats to plants, animals and ecosystems remain and extinctions caused by human activities continue at an alarming rate. To meet these ongoing challenges, members of the Convention met in London in 2003. The meeting was called '2010 – The Global Diversity Challenge'. At the meeting, participants pledged to reduce the current rate of biodiversity loss at the national, regional and global level by 2010.

A participant of the sixth conference of the Convention on Biological Diversity studies a section of an 1158-year-old Douglas tree that was on display at the conference in April 2002.

Practical results

Since signing the Convention, governments around the world have worked to combine conservation and development. Governments are also working to educate people and raise awareness about the importance of plant diversity and the need to conserve it. In Mexico, farmers now plant coffee trees individually instead of in massive plantations that reduce the biodiversity of the area. These farmers can then rely entirely on natural predators to control pests rather than use chemical pesticides.

A farmer checks to see if coffee berries are ready to be picked.

Celebrating the Earth's biodiversity

Every year, the International Day for Biological Diversity takes place on 22 May. Participating countries like the UK hold activities that aim to increase public understanding and awareness of biodiversity issues. These activities, often aimed at younger generations, stress the importance of biodiversity. They explain the effects that biodiversity loss has on everyday life, and what people can do to help preserve the Earth's habitats and wildlife.

Texas rigs-to-reefs

The state of Texas, in the USA, has a coastline of 591 kilometres (367 miles) along the Gulf of Mexico. Its local economy has benefited greatly from the huge reservoirs of petroleum that lie below the seabed of the Gulf. It is one of the country's leading oil-producing and refining states. It is also an important producer of natural gas. Today, there are more than 4000 oil and gas rigs in the Gulf of Mexico. Many of them stand in the shallow waters off the Texas coast.

Rigs of life

Almost immediately after an oil or gas rig has been positioned in the Gulf, organisms like corals and sponges attach themselves to it. These organisms attract other species including sea urchins, fish and large predators like sharks. Endangered sea turtles like Kemp's Ridley turtles are also attracted to the rich feeding areas that surround the rig. The rig provides shelter from water currents and becomes a protected breeding ground. The longer the rig is in place, the more developed the underwater ecosystem becomes.

This marine biologist is checking the condition of an underwater artificial reef. Coral and underwater plants have already started to grow on the artificial reef.

The Texas Artificial Reef Program

In 1989, the Texas authorities passed the Artificial Reef Act. The aim of the Act was to promote, develop and maintain artificial reefs in Texas. The Texas Rigs-to-Reefs Program officially began in 1990. Rigs-to-reefs is the term used to describe the conversion of oil and gas rigs that are no longer in use into artificial offshore reefs. Under the Rigs-to-Reefs Program, companies can donate their unused rigs to be used as artificial reefs instead of having to remove them from the Gulf. The companies also donate to the Program 50 per cent of the money they save by leaving the rigs in place. To date, oil and gas companies have donated 49 rigs to the Texas Rigs-to-Reefs Program.

A rig being towed back to land so it can be dismantled. Before the Texas Rigs-to-Reefs Program began, oil and gas companies had to remove a rig from the Texas coast within a year of it no longer being in use.

A win-win situation

The people of Texas also benefit from the rich habitat provided by the artificial reefs. By providing food and shelter, the reefs can help regenerate overfished populations of reef fish. As a result, the reefs offer recreational and commercial fishing and excellent diving opportunities. The artificial reefs also maintain the important marine ecosystems that were established when the rigs were first installed.

The three methods used to convert a rig into an artificial reef.

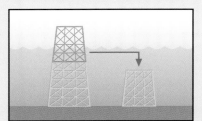

The partial-removal method

The topple-and-place method

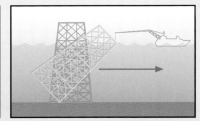

The tow-and-place method

Saving the UK's peat bogs

A peat bog in Yorkshire, the UK.

Peat is a thick layer of partly rotted vegetation which has built up in wet, airless conditions over many centuries. Peat **bogs** are an important ecosystem because they remove **carbon dioxide** (CO_2) from the atmosphere and then store it. In the UK, 90 per cent of all peat bogs have been lost over the last 100 years. As a result, they are now one of the UK's rarest habitats. The animal and plant species that make their home in the bogs are also increasingly threatened. These include the ground-nesting nightjar and plants like sphagnum moss and great sundew.

Bogs in danger

People have always made use of peat bogs. They have been drained and reclaimed for agriculture, planted for forestry and dug up for fuel. Some of the UK's most important peat bogs are Hatfield Moor and Thorne Moor in Yorkshire and Wedholme Flow in Cumbria. In the 1950s, the UK government gave commercial companies permission to gather peat for use as a fuel or as garden compost. Since the 1960s, the UK's remaining areas of peat bogs have come under growing threat due to the increasingly intensive methods used to cut peat and increasing demand for peat. By the 1990s, over two-thirds of the peat used in the UK was bought by gardeners.

Working together

In 1990, conservation organizations formed the Peatlands Campaign Consortium. Its aim was to protect the UK's remaining peat bogs. As a result of its campaigns, major Do-It-Yourself stores and garden centres agreed not to sell peat from peat bogs that have been protected. Sixty-six local authorities also signed the Wildlife Trusts' Peatland Protection Charter promising not to use peat.

Following further campaigning, the UK government awarded Special Area of Conservation status to the country's three largest remaining peat bogs – Hatfield Moor, Thorne Moor and Wedholme Flow – in 2000. In February 2002, the government announced that peat cutting would stop immediately at Thorne and Wedholme moors and by autumn 2004 at Hatfield Moor.

Peat cut from the UK's dwindling peat bogs is dried so it can be used as fuel or garden compost.

Finding alternatives

The Consortium, along with other wildlife groups, is now encouraging gardeners to use alternatives to peat. Major peat companies are also looking into alternatives for peat. Organizations such as the National Trust and government bodies are also phasing out the use of peat on their lands.

Lindow Man

In 1984, workmen cutting peat in Lindow Moss in the UK found the well-preserved body of a man. Archaeologists discovered that the body, known as Lindow Man, was 2000 years old. The water in peat bogs is **acidic** and very few bacteria can live in such a condition. This means that the decomposition of animals, trees and pollen slows down. Discoveries like Lindow Man are important to archaeologists and historians because they provide information about environmental change and about the food, clothes and customs of past cultures.

When Lindow Man was first discovered, scientists and local police originally thought that he had died recently because his body was so well preserved.

Global citizens

Habitats all over the world are threatened with destruction due to logging, clearing, fragmentation, the introduction of invasive species and over-harvesting. When habitats are destroyed, many animal and plant species become threatened or even driven to extinction. We lose important food sources and opportunities for recreation and tourism. We also lose valuable resources like timber and plants that can be used to make medicines. In recent years, non-governmental organizations (NGOs) like the World Wide Fund for Nature and governments worldwide have recognized the importance of protecting the Earth's habitats.

Reversing habitat destruction

It is possible to reverse some of the damage caused to habitats. This can be done by replanting trees and plants and re-introducing the animals that used to inhabit an area. But habitat restoration requires years of commitment and hard work. Today, many countries have risen to the challenge and are now trying to restore damaged habitats. Local communities in Gazi Bay, Kenya, have worked to restore the district's mangrove forests by planting over 300,000 mangrove trees in areas that had been cleared for industry.

Local people plant young trees in the threatened rainforests of Madagascar. Scientists estimate that about 90 per cent of the island's forests have disappeared.

The Mediterranean Basin covers an area of 2,362,000 square kilometres (911,970 square miles). Deciduous forests used to cover much of this region. Today, only 111,000 square kilometres (42,860 square miles) of these forests remain. As part of an effort to conserve this vegetation, countries within the region have set up inland and coastal parks, reserves and other protected areas.

Conserving the Earth's hotspots

In 2000, a group of international organizations concerned about the environment launched the Critical Ecosystem Partnership Fund. This fund of US$150 million is designed to protect the world's 25 hotspots for future generations. In its first year, the Fund focused on the hotspot regions of the Mediterranean Basin, Madagascar, West Africa and the Tropical Andes. The Fund aims to study at least five additional hotspots per year. By providing money and technical help, the Fund works with non-governmental organizations and communities to save the unique and rich plant and animal life in such hotspots.

Sustainable development

If we regulate the use of natural resources, it should be possible to maintain our current rate of development while still preserving and conserving the world's habitats so future generations have access to the same resources that we do. But there are many challenges to achieving this aim. Some large companies and even governments do not agree that there is any need for regulation, especially when a habitat contains valuable resources that can provide jobs and income for people. We must somehow balance our economic, environmental and social needs against the value of our natural habitats.

In a nutshell

Habitats are threatened by: • land clearing • fragmentation • over-exploitation • introduction of new species • pollution • natural disasters such as lightning, storms and volcanic eruptions.

The destruction of habitats results in the loss of: • biological diversity • resources such as wood, water and food • areas or environments in which people have lived for generations • areas used for recreational purposes • plants with potential medicinal properties • clean air • clean water.

What can I do?

Help to conserve our environment! We can all do our part to protect the Earth's precious habitats and wildlife. Here are some ways you can help.

Listen to the experts

- Invite members of local environmental groups to come to your school to talk about how they protect the Earth's habitats and plant and animal species.

- Write an essay on what you have learned. If your school has its own newspaper or newsletter, write an article about the talk.

Learn about your planet and environment

- Learn more about the environment you live in and the various habitats around your home from newspapers, books and websites.

Get involved

- Join an organization that works to protect or clean up habitats, such as the World Wide Fund for Nature (http://panda.org).

- Stop junk mail coming into your home. Write to Mailing Preference Service, DMA House, 70 Margaret Street, London W1W 8SS, and tell them that you do not wish to receive such mail. This will reduce your family's junk mail by up to 75 per cent, saving up to 1.5 trees per person per year. You can also reach them at www.mpsonline.org.uk.

Going on school trips to nearby gardens or forests is one way of learning more about the environment you live in.

These women are part of an environmental group that has volunteered to clean up Huntington Beach in California in the USA.

Clean up your environment

Why not help to clean up an area in your local community? This could be your school grounds or a nearby area such as a park or forest. By doing so, you will improve a local wildlife habitat and create a cleaner open space. It will also give you the chance to learn about the habitat and the plants and animals that live there.

- As a class, decide which area you think needs to be cleaned up. If you plan to clean a public area, ask your teacher to help you get permission from the local authority or site owner.
- Work with your classmates to list the most common types of rubbish that you expect to find while you are cleaning up.
- Remember to bring in clean-up supplies like gloves and rubbish bags on your clean-up day.
- On Clean-up Day, in groups, clear up the area that has been assigned to you. Be careful not to pick up any sharp objects, such as broken glass. If you find something sharp, ask your teacher or an adult for help.
- Make a list of the rubbish that you find.
- When you get back to your classroom, compare the two lists that you made. Discuss in your group where the rubbish items that you picked up might have come from.
- Remember to take a 'before' and 'after' photograph of the area.

Only leave footprints

- When you go for a walk in the countryside with your family, just enjoy it. Do not gather wildflowers to decorate your home or collect frogspawn or insects like butterflies. Leave the wildlife in its proper habitat. Also when you are walking, always try to follow well-worn paths so you do not disturb the wildlife living there. Do not drop litter. Take your rubbish home or find a proper litter bin to put it in.

Glossary

acidic substance with a sour taste. Strong acids can dissolve even metal.

alien species plant or animal that moves from its original habitat into a new area

amino acid substance containing nitrogen and hydrogen which is found in proteins and which occurs naturally in plants and animals

autotroph plant or algae that can produce its own food using the Sun's energy; also known as a producer

biodiversity number of different plant and animal species that are present within a given area

biome major geographic region that contains a specific community of plants, animals and other organisms

bleaching process that removes colour from substances

bog soft, wet ground with earth made up mainly of decayed matter

bushel unit of volume that is used to measure agricultural produce like corn or beans

carbon dioxide colourless gas in the Earth's atmosphere that consists of two oxygen atoms and one carbon atom; carbon dioxide helps trap heat close to the Earth

chlorophyll green pigment needed by plants to trap light energy and make food

chronic severe and lasting for a long time

colony group of animals, birds or insects that lives together

Convention group of organizations that shares a common interest

crustacean animal with a hard shell and several pairs of legs that usually lives in water, such as crabs and shrimps

cultivate grow plants for a special purpose

delta area of low, flat land where a river splits and spreads out into several branches before entering the sea

drought prolonged lack of rainfall

ecosystem community of plants and animals in a physical environment

equator imaginary line around the middle of the Earth at an equal distance from the north and south poles

evaporation change from a liquid or solid into gas

evolve develop over time

extinct exists no more; dead

fossil fuel fuel derived from the fossilized remains of plants and animals. Examples of fossil fuels are coal and petroleum.

genetic diversity variation found within a species, which is the result of breeding between individuals over a wide area

groundwater fresh water that is found beneath the surface of the ground

habitat natural home of an animal or a plant

heterotroph organism that cannot produce its own food; also known as a consumer

home range limited area within which an individual animal finds its food, reproduces and lives

inbreeding repeated breeding of closely related animals

indigenous belongs naturally to a particular area

infrastructure basic facilities of a country such as transport systems, power plants and roads

invasive species alien species that disrupts the normal functioning and/or structure of an ecosystem

irrigate supply water to agricultural land by artificial means

lava molten rock that is thrown out by a volcano from deep below the Earth

migratory travelling from one habitat to another in order to mate or find food

mollusc invertebrate that has no backbone and a soft body that is protected by a hard shell

monoculture landscape in which one species completely, or almost completely, dominates

mudflat area of flat empty land at the coast that is covered by the sea only when the tide is in

native species that occurs naturally in an area

nutrient substance that helps plants and animals grow

organism living thing such as a plant, animal, fungi or bacteria

parched extremely dry

photosynthesize use light energy to make food from carbon dioxide and water. Only green plants photosynthesize because they have chlorophyll.

pollinate transfer pollen from the stamen (male part) to the ovule (female part) of a plant. This process is important for coniferous and flowering plants to reproduce.

precipitation water that falls to the Earth as rain, snow, sleet or hail

predator animal that hunts and kills other animals

protein part of food that is essential for all plants and animals

salinity amount of salt in a body of water

sediment fine material like dust that is deposited by winds, glaciers and rivers and then settles on the ocean bed

spawn in fish, the act of mating and releasing fertilized eggs

species group of animals or plants whose members can interbreed and produce fertile offspring

sub-tropical characterized by a warm and humid climate, often near tropical regions

sustainable able to renew itself

temperate climatic zone characterized by mild weather and distinct seasons

terrestrial land based

tract very large area of land

transitional changing from one state to another

vapour tiny drops of water, or other liquids, in the air

Finding out more

Books:

Earth Files: Rivers and Lakes, Chris Oxlade (Heinemann Library, 2003)

Green Files: Wildlife in Danger, Steve Parker (Heinemann Library, 2003)

Just the Facts: Global Population, Paul Brown (Heinemann Library, 2002)

The Life of Plants: Plant Habitats, Louise and Richard Spilsbury (Heinemann Library, 2002)

Taking Action: World Wide Fund for Nature, Louise Spilsbury (Heinemann Library, 2000)

Videos:

The Coral Reef: A Living Wonder, AIMS Multimedia (1995)

Creatures of the Mangrove, National Geographic (1998)

Discovery Channel School Science: Habitats of the World, Discovery Channel Video (1997)

Ecosystems for Children: All About Forest Ecosystems, Schlessinger Media (2001)

Freshwater Ecosystems. Biomes of the World in Action: Freshwater Ecosystems, Schlessinger Media (2001)

Plant Life in Action: Plant Biodiversity, Schlessinger Media (2000)

Websites:

Foundation for Global Biodiversity Education for Children
http://www.globiokids.org/

Life on Earth
http://edugreen.teri.res.in/explore/life/life.htm

World Wildlife Fund
http://www.worldwildlife.org/fun/kids.cfm

Young People's Trust for the Environment
http://www.yptenc.org.uk/

Organizations:

Conservation International
1919 M Street, NW Suite 600
Washington, D.C. 20036
USA
Phone: 202 912 1000
http://www.conservation.org

Environment Australia
John Gorton Building, King Edward Terrace
Parkes ACT 2600
GPO Box 787
Canberra ACT 2601
Australia
Phone: 61 2 6274 1111
Fax: 61 2 6274 1666
http://www.ea.gov.au

Marine Conservation Society
Unit 3, Wolf Business Park, Alton Road
Ross-on-Wye, Herefordshire HR9 5NB
UK
Phone: 01989 566017
http://www.mcsuk.org/

WWF-UK
Panda House, Weyside Park
Godalming,
Surrey GU7 1XR
UK
Phone: 01483 426444
Fax: 01483 426409
http://www.wwf-uk.org

Disclaimer: All the Internet addresses (URLs) given in this book were valid at the time of going to press. However, due to the dynamic nature of the Internet, some addresses may have changed or sites may have changed or ceased to exist since publication. While the author and Publisher regret any inconvenience this may cause readers, no responsibility for any such changes can be accepted by either the author or the Publisher.

Index